praise for
What the Body Already Knows

K.E. Ogden's stunning chapbook, *What the Body Already Knows*, is a journey through grief for a father who "hung the sun" and a troubled mother who lives in memory as "fingerprints in the tops of all those biscuits." Every poem is rooted in the world of the body—of those we love, of the earth, and of the sea, where the poet surprises herself by "singing underwater," a perfect metaphor for what Ogden's poetry accomplishes: a music all her own, rising, above all odds, from sorrow's depths.

Rebecca McClanahan
Author of *In the Key of New York City* and *The Tribal Knot*

Every once in a precious while, a book comes into my life that shakes me out of my long days and worries, one that offers me honesty and real connection to its author. K.E. Ogden's new collection of poetry, *What the Body Already Knows*, is exactly that kind of book. These poems provide an atlas of loss, both to it and away from it, line by line. Whether telling the story of a mother lost in her sleep, a day lost to rumination over the corpse of a deer, or an entire year lost to loss itself, these poems show a way through it all. Yes, there is pain here, and fear, hospital rooms, and heavy memories from hard days, but these poems are much more than specimens lined up as examples of troubles in a drawer. They are alive, and colorful, and covered in all manner of beauty to render life's real value.

Jack B. Bedell
Author of *Color All Maps New*
Poet Laureate, State of Louisiana, 2017-2019

K. E. Ogden's *What the Body Already Knows* begins with a father highlighting for his daughter the way out. Of course there is no way out. This collection chronicles the "year of forgot to breathe," the year both parents die. In a pastoral scene, we see the pond filled with tires and truck parts, the pond where they throw in a dead deer on the count of three. These harsh, beautiful poems stun us with honesty, grit, and transformation.

Peggy Shumaker
Author of *CAIRN* and *Gnawed Bones*

The skillful and heartfelt elegies of Kirsten Ogden's *What the Body Already Knows* show us the whole world—its people and elements and animals—in dynamic mourning. In poems about the terror and splendor of life passing, of losing parents, of finding new anxieties and new joys in parenthood, Ogden's voice is at times lyrical and at times irreverent, but always well rendered and always humane: 'When I woke this morning, I wasn't yet / an orphan.' The poet restlessly seeks "synonyms for grief" in her crisp language and startling figurations. Even in the face of loss, Ogden reminds us the world is fragile, but the world is beautiful.

Richie Hofmann
Author of *A Hundred Lovers* and *Second Empire*

What the Body Already Knows reminds us that grief does not have just one form. It is not just solid, not just emotional terrain, not just morphing bodies & time, it takes every form of matter. Ogden's work asks us to break open the cycles we come from & to be among grief's great disruption to our relational rhythms. How when our people go beyond, especially parents/parental figures, they don't leave, but how we are with each other becomes new. How in the midst of great grief comes change where we find new selves. The language in this book creates striking & surprising landscapes. Ogden's uses of form & symbolism build meditations on duality & coupling in the midst of transition. This simmering collection asks us to pull up a chair to grief's wake, welcome the deviations that arise & change the cycles we claim for ourselves.

Nabila Lovelace
Author of *Sons of Achilles*

These elegiac poems are invitations to the poet's living history in the present moment, where memory, emotion, and the outside world intertwine. This storytelling in lyric form reveals Ogden's exceptional dexterity in line-handling and imagery, most notable where the mundane and surreal collide. This debut chapbook introduces a powerful and engaging new voice to hear and follow.

Lauri Scheyer
Author of *A History of African American Poetry*

Kirsten Ogden's poems offer synonyms for grief while building new worlds simultaneously. These lyrical stanzas map the bridge between generations, and the forgotten wooden steps that take you home again. Cutting through the fog and the noise of the nightbirds, Ogden's poetry wields the capacity to sketch the unseen shadows on the horizon. She even sings back to them.

Mike Sonksen
Author of *Letters to my City*

K.E. Ogden's *What the Body Already Knows* manifests the circular and cyclical nature of grief with stunning directness and clarity. These poems are "muckings of primordial mud," yet amazingly they give words to what cannot be said. Ogden examines the wreckage of loss, and these parts are "scooped up to make a new world." I have never thought of loss as a mirror before reading these poems, but grief in this collection becomes a way of seeing the self in a world forever changed.

Adam Clay
Author of *To Make Room for the Sea*

What the Body Already Knows

poems
K.E. Ogden

Finishing Line Press
Georgetown, Kentucky

WHAT THE BODY ALREADY KNOWS.
Copyright © 2022 by K.E. Ogden.

ISBN 978-1-64662-956-5 First Edition
All rights reserved under International and Pan-American Copyright Conventions. No part of this book may be reproduced in any manner whatsoever without written permission from the publisher, except in the case of brief quotations embodied in critical articles and reviews.

Cover and interior art by Kiyoshi Nakazawa
Cover and interior design by Mathew Digges

Publisher: Leah Huete de Maines
Editor: Christen Kincaid

Order online: www.finishinglinepress.com
also available on amazon.com

Author inquiries and mail orders:
Finishing Line Press
PO Box 1626
Georgetown, Kentucky 40324
USA

for the grandmothers,
 Alice Rose and Irma Lee

CONTENTS

1.

Mapping the Route / 13
Kicker Rock / 14
Darwin's Finches / 15
The Hungriest Moth / 17
Synonyms for Grief / 18
The Extra / 21
The Great Sphinx / 22
The 34th Year / 25

2.

What the Body Already Knows / 28
Fruit Stand / 30
Singing Underwater / 31
Piranha Fishing / 32
Mother's Wings / 34
Like That / 36
Aubade at the Kitchen Table / 37
Hush / 38

Notes & Acknowledgements / 40
Gratitudes & Love / 41

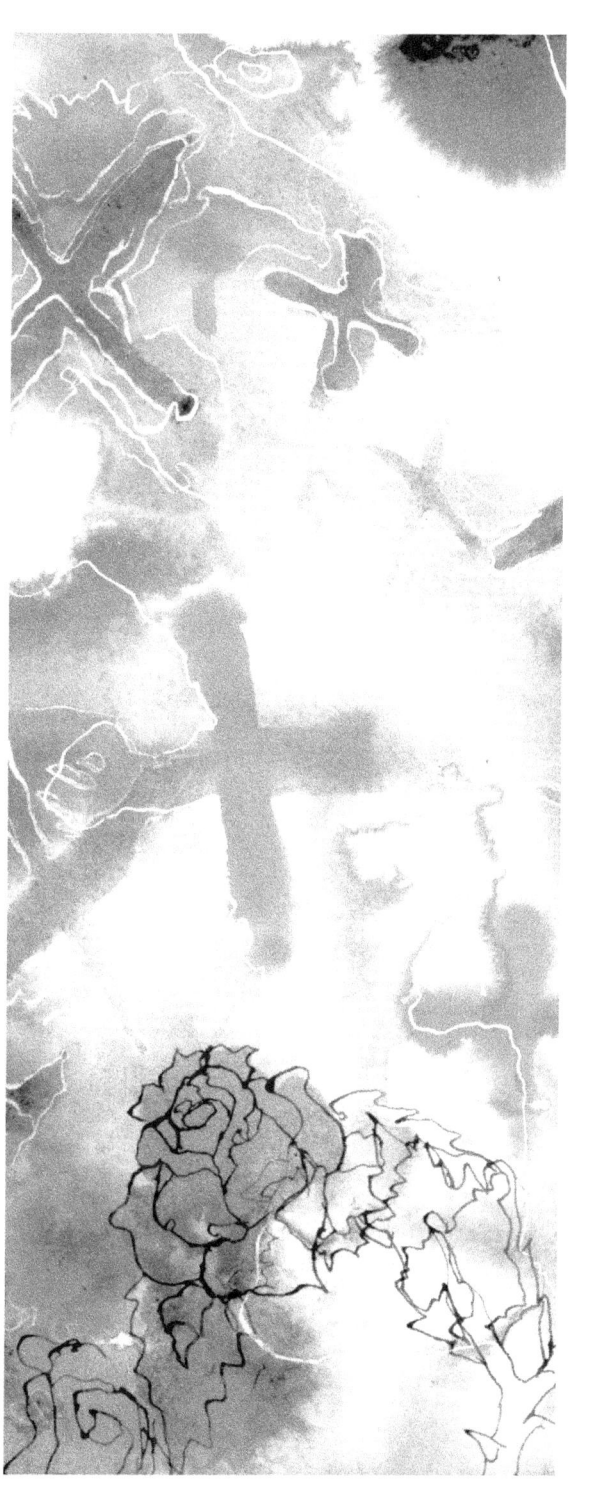

1.

MAPPING THE ROUTE

I've been driving for miles heading north
away from air thick with rain, my pockets full
of foil-wrapped biscuits smeared in strawberry jam
and bacon bits. The blacktop is rotting
copperhead. The open atlas on the dash
is marked in orange highlighter by my father.
This is the route away from home, he said,
still smelling of sawdust and pine sap.
I step on the gas. My callused feet can walk
a hot gravel road all the way to the pond
and into the muddy banks where we once saw
a deer swollen with gnats and bees.
It all meant something else when I was younger,
that dead doe a signal to let go, to surrender
each prayer to the sky, to the cornrows,
to the catfish scumming the surface
of the pond where we threw tires
and old truck parts. Where we threw
that deer on the count of three,
then headed back to the porch swing
and slurped coffee until the heat took us all.

KICKER ROCK

It juts from the water like two rotting teeth.
From the sand, we stare out across

the blue expanse of San Cristobal.
This is the place you are dying.

Frigate birds swoop above,
their angled wings like pterodactyls.

Your grave is a broken, seasick thing.
When I woke this morning, I wasn't yet

an orphan. Soon I'll run my hands
across the rock's bird-shit surface.

Darwin says each slight variation
is preserved by natural selection.

I am still here, then, a deviation.
We circulate in one another's blood.

DARWIN'S FINCHES

Father kept two finches in a cage
suspended above the archway

marking off the dining room
of our small apartment.

Walking beneath the suspended cage
felt like moving from one realm

to the next. In bird collections,
long drawers are lined

with feathery bird skins
arranged from fattest to smallest,

tummies up, beaks the tip
of arrowed bodies, tails tagged,

souls released. I listen for my father's
warbling message but hear only

muckings of primordial mud
scooped up to make a new world.

THE HUNGRIEST MOTH

In silk-spun tents spanning clusters of branches,
Gypsy Moths eat through my sleep. The summer
Father died, they died by the hundreds. Tree fungus.
The frozen, milk-beige moths blackened trunks
until songbirds plucked them. To keep my father alive,
I arrange questions around his bed like graceful ghosts.
I swallow stones and hope I'll sink. He and I walk
the cemeteries and find bald trees, roots dug up
with jackhammers. We saw a young girl fall asleep
in the forest. The Gypsy Moths webbed her mouth,
her eyes. Their cocoons were tethered hot-air balloons
waving from tree tops. After my father died,
I roamed his house looking for him. I found letters,
a handkerchief, a wallet, his teeth. I took it all.
Some nights I return to where the girl hatched
and I perform experiments. I see white teeth
in each cocoon. If I cut little squares into my body,
Father, could you look inside to see if I'm moving?

SYNONYMS FOR GRIEF

Daddy used to cup his hands at my ear
so I could hear the river. Every time

the world stops, something is lost.
A field of dogs shouts at the deer

in the dark trees. Empty skynight.
We buried the pig in a pit and now

we're standing around the fire
with cans of Bud. Pull off one ear

and then another. These are synonyms
for grief: door, dirt, potato salad,

whiskey, cigarettes, shovel, biscuits,
pine logs, fried chicken, cigarette smoke,

grits, porch. That big wild Oak tree.
That Pecan tree with its lightning-split trunk

still giving seed. This is a name
for sadness: a mechanical butterfly

caught in a jar, and if you press
this button, it will push again and again

against the glass. Open the door.
Beneath the door, beneath that space

in the door, no gravity. People speak
in thought balloons. Daddy said,

When I die just throw me in the ditch.

THE EXTRA

I have called this morning unto myself.

It's the birds that get me up so early—
the cats clicking their teeth to the music.

When the coroner's office called
they offered to show me mother's body.

You'll want to pay the extra fee for make-up,
says the lady on the phone. *Believe me it helps.*

Mother died in her bed.
They found the cat sleeping on her chest.

A homeless woman living with her
called me the day after my birthday.

She told me not to bother.
You don't wanna remember her that way.

But I wanted to see. I wanted to kiss her.
Out my window the displaced, famous

Pasadena parrots scream from an arrow in the sky.
Mother's cat clicks its teeth. I did pay the extra.

THE GREAT SPHINX

In the last letter she wrote:
>*I am getting older. It's becoming too late
>to do anything of consequence.*

Just like that.
Giving up so easy.

In a scrapbook there's a photo of me I love:
My birthday at Grandma's. I'm turning four.
I'm wearing a blue shift dress with white lines
marking my body into boxes.

An eyelet collar squares each shoulder.
White knee socks. Shiny black shoes. I am a catalogue
girl with the whole world in front of me!

Hand on my hip, big smile,
pink and red party hat on my head.

In her last letter she wrote about the Great Sphinx:
>*It weighs more than an asteroid!
>It was built 5000 years ago!*

I'm wringing my hands because I'm afraid of death.
> *Tell me how you started putting butter in*
> *your coffee,*
is what she writes next. Then
> *Last night I dreamt of a pan full of sizzling*
> *piranhas, teeth shivering in their steaming mouths.*

I think we should all be standing on our forepaws,
looking over the head of the Sphinx
to see what's out there.

It's hailing golf balls here today!
I'll bet it's sunny where you are.

My daughter calls to say she's made it
to her play rehearsal early.
Everyone is eating birthday cake, she says.

THE 34TH YEAR

Blacked out year of the undone:
clothes-washing, cat box cleaning, bill-
paying. Year of forgot to breathe. No breathing.
Heaving muscles through a sieve. Dead
ivy sliding along gutters to a piss-drenched ocean.
Abandoned cats, one with its ear torn off, belly distended,
another limping, its entrails uncoiled.

> The year mother held up her breast
> and they took it. I didn't notice I'd
> disappeared. The year father's pancreas
> went rotten. Year of black

holes. Tantrum year. Stirring along the banks
near the deep river. X'd out, marked out, blackout year.
Virgin scars rising to the surfaces. Paper-thin memory.
Benumbed year of pushing through.

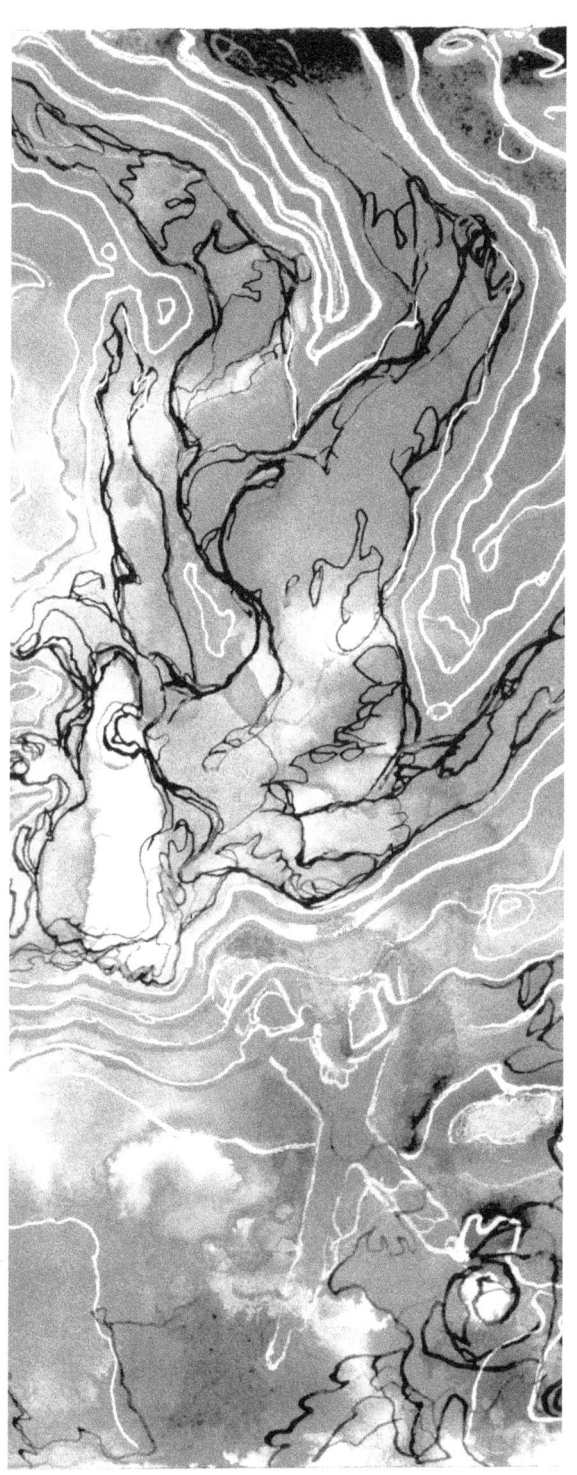

2.

WHAT THE BODY ALREADY KNOWS

I'm thinking of that last time we watched tennis
from your hospital bed. Your wife in the other room

packing for Kentucky. I didn't have to ask you
what madness possessed her. The body

always makes its choices without us. You knew
you wouldn't ever see the blue line of trees

at the crossing place. But you let her do it anyway
wrap wine glasses in newspaper, placing them

in boxes so the stems stayed strong. I was leaving,
too, already packed and aware of the hours.

Is it safe to say you lived a good life? What is this all
except a kind of fear forgotten in each serve

across a net, each foot over the line?
We drank frozen coffees. Your eyes were as blue

as they'd ever been. When I left, you held
your palm in the air. I got into my car

and didn't look back. Weeks later, after you'd gone,
I was in a dinghy with an oxygen tank strapped

to my back. Our guide said sharks aren't dangerous.
When my body folded into the water,

it was colder than I thought it would be.
The current carried me towards a channel;

I curled into that stillness of black water.
There I watched sharks swim in perfect lines.

I thought of you calling out to the television
that last afternoon: *Go! Go! Go!*

FRUIT STAND

When we reach San Cristobal
we are chili peppers.

A woman sells green and red
tomatoes, smiling at us

with black teeth. A baby
milks her breast. A boy spins

a top on a piece of cardboard.
It's been weeks since I've had fresh fruit.

The tomatoes are hard and shiny.
The boy is missing three

fingers on his left hand. Over
and over again, he tries to spin the top

until it whirs and dances.
I kneel and steady his thumb

and pinkie. We flick together.
When I was about his age

you told me storks bring babies.
I imagined myself carried to you

in a cloth hammock
dangling from the beak.

I give the woman my money
and bite. The skin splits

and juice runs down my hand.

SINGING UNDERWATER

When Daddy died I was swimming with sharks in the
        Galapagos.

I surprised myself by singing underwater.
I write an X on my wrists when I need to stay alive.

Were his eyes green like mine?
If I could say something else I would say: X.

The last time I saw him was in June.
I curled into his body and laid my head on his chest.

He sang, covered in sawdust and diesel:
Hello daughter. Blood of my blood. It's a wonderful day.
        It's your birthday.

I move my body toward the plume cloud as it dissipates.

His death: the way bat wings curl and the body gets chalky.
The body stiff and rubbery.

Just inches from an open window.
Daddy cut down trees and hauled them to the mill.

He came home with pine dust in his chest hair.
He hung the sun.

PIRANHA FISHING

Your wife tells me I should write your obituary;

>*You've got the writing talent.*

>>I want this as a compliment,
>>or some kindness, but I always thought
>>her a bitch.

Here: rustling leaves sound like rain,
or bubbling Piranha.

>>Father, you read this from my guidebook.
>>*Logo Panacocha,* you say, a place
>>I did not visit despite your urgings.

>>I cannot say I'm sorry
>>even if they're surprisingly easy to catch,
>>and *make a fine meal.*

I might've brought back a jawbone
and kept it in colored glass
but I'm not much for fishing.

>>Can you see, Father?
>>Two birds flit among the
>>branches.

I'm back home.

    Remember Rich's poem after his father
    died of cancer?

    He wrote how his mother's ashes
    were gritty and yellowed,
    heavy with chunks of bone,
    but his father's ashes, silt.

MOTHER'S WINGS

Because the rain came and the roads were slick and I thought of you commuting to work.

Because the night can hum so loud sometimes that I can't hear your voice.

Because the night can hum so quiet sometimes that I can only hear your voice.

Because your false teeth slipped into your margarita right after your divorce and I pretended not to notice.

Because I'm happy the lump in your breast was only a cyst that first time.

Because I liked the way you smiled when I said you weren't crazy.

Because you left him when you were 21 and pregnant a third time.

Because your voice on the phone was full of smoke and coffee and a new man.

Because you let me take your arm when you stumbled up the wooden steps.

Because I heard you laugh over the phone when I knew you were crying.

Because you took my face in your hands and I felt your calluses rub my cheeks.

Because late that night you called and asked me to come through the hot air.

Because I watched you bathe and dry your new breast.

Because you longed to fly.

Because you stood on a cliff and looked across the desert and spread your arms.

Because I saw you leap and take to the wind.

LIKE THAT

My hands do not belong to my body. They reach to touch Mama's shoulders. I am prepared to bleed: the rude half-light working me every night at 3:34 am. City lights, helicopters and cheap blinds. And storm too. It takes the light out of the room. Takes me back home.

I'd run my hands inside the rib cages of other people.

When Mama died it was two days after my birthday. The woman on the phone said *She's gone, baby.* Like that.

Thunder road. Mama's fingerprints in the tops of all those biscuits. Hands bigger than her whole body at the end of it all.

AUBADE AT THE KITCHEN TABLE

My daughter is at her rehearsal
learning blocking marks for *James and the Giant Peach*.

My coffee has gone cold, milk filmed
across the top in a thin shroud.

I am as old as my mother was when she died.

There are no doctors rushing me in a gurney
towards an operating room. No IV fluids. No tubes
connecting me to this world.

It isn't too late, I tell myself.
The sun may widen its lines to reach me.

HUSH

One of my high school students read it in the paper,
last week in San Antonio a woman was charged
with murdering her three-week-old son.

She dismembered the baby's body with a knife
and two swords. She tore off the face,
chewed three baby toes before stabbing herself.

I take to the freeways listening to talk radio.
Light rises over my city as I drive east. Yesterday,
a boy in some other country walked into a marketplace

swaddled in explosives. He was crying for his mother,
inconsolable. I drive with the windows down.
Hair whirls and whips, stings my face.

A director being interviewed explains his artistic
process as *seeing the present*. He confesses to using
homeless and deranged people in his latest movie

for realism. Sometimes I sleep in late. I relearn
green: grass, leaves, lichen. I relearn soil after a long rain,
thick mud full of ants and winged termites.

I relearn shadow, then light, their interplay along
the horizon. I relearn shapes: a circle, for instance,
larger or smaller by choice, room to widen.

Tonight I bathe and rest. I cut leeks and potatoes.
When I sit outside, I drink wine and try to make out
constellations: the phoenix, the winged horse.

I watch until fog crawls around the bend, rising up
into the trees. The temperature drops. Nightbirds
call to me from the sky.

NOTES

"The 34th Year" is after a poem by Andrew Grace

"Synonyms for Grief" is dedicated to Jake Adam York

"The Great Sphinx" is for Nancy Zafris

"What the Body Already Knows" is dedicated to my step-father, Ted Gregg, and references "If My Head Hurt a Hair's Foot" by Dylan Thomas

"Piranha Fishing" references a poem by Rich Yurman, "Ashes," from the book *Giraffe*, March Street Press, 2002

"Hush" is for Zach Savich with thanks to Samantha N. Simpson

ACKNOWLEDGEMENTS

I am grateful to the editors of the following publications where some of these poems first appeared, sometimes in altered form with alternate titles:
Arsenic Lobster
Avatar Review
Fringe
Kenyon Review Online

Special acknowledgement to Austin Veldman, editor-in-chief and founder of Twyckenham Notes for honoring 4 of these poems with Honorable Mention in the 2021 Joe Bolton Poetry Contest: *Kicker Rock; The Hungriest Moth; The Great Sphinx; The 34th year.*

GRATITUDES & LOVE

After James Baldwin: "Love takes off the masks we fear we cannot live without and know we cannot live within."

Thank you, readers, for supporting independent presses and small publishers for the work they do to keep poetry alive in the world. Thank you for spending time with my poems. I'm so grateful.

My deepest appreciation and thank you to the Staff at *Finishing Line Press* for giving this chapbook a home and for their hard work and support. My heartfelt gratitude to FLP Director Leah Maines for championing work by women – and especially for calling me on my birthday to let me know about this great honor of winning the *New Women's Voices* Chapbook Contest. Thanks to Kevin Maines and Christen Kincaid for all of your help and guidance with this publishing project.

My heartfelt love and gratitude to my friend Maggie Smith for her generous and brilliant insight and attention to these poems and to this chapbook. Special love and humble thanks to my friends and champions who gave feedback on individual poems and on early drafts: Adam Clay, Andrew Grace, Richie Hofmann, Geeta Kothari, Samantha Simpson, July Westhale, the great W. David Hall, and the great, late Jake Adam York.

Thank you to my teachers and mentors for the love they've given me throughout my life: Mrs. Carrick and Mrs. Moore, my elementary teachers who always let me turn in poems for my projects and cultivated my love for language; my high school teachers – the late Dean Christianson –"Mr.C" and Abe "Doc" Doctolero, without whom this first-gen kid never would've thought about college; my community college professors Katherine Harer and the late Rich Yurman for your love and guidance and for telling me my voice mattered; Jack Bedell, my undergraduate mentor and professor, for pushing me to write during a very challenging time in my life and beyond; to my teachers at UAF, especially Peggy Shumaker, and the late Roy K. Bird; my dissertation director at LSU, Les Wade, who helped me see that creativity is a form of scholarship.

I am indebted to the Village of Gambier, Ohio and to the Kenyon Review for providing me with a writing family for the last 15 years. You welcomed me as a Peter Taylor poetry fellow, an instructor in the Young Writers at Kenyon program, a poet laureate of Gambier, and a founding contributor to the Kenyon Review blog. I am especially grateful to: David Lynn, Anna Duke Reach, Tyler Meier, Sergei Lobanov-Rostavsky, and my mentor and big brother W. David Hall. Thank you to my instructors in the KR adult writers workshops: Rebecca McClanahan, David Baker, Geeta Kothari, Brad Kessler; thank you to my fellow teachers in the Kenyon Review Young Writers program over the years, especially Samantha Simpson, Andy Grace, Tory Weber, Julia Grawemeyer, Liz Forman, Tyler Meier, Richie Hofmann, Nabila Lovelace, Noah Falck, Adam Clay, Paige Wilson, Miriam Walden, and so many more. You all became the family I needed most. Thank you to my former students in the young writers program over the years. I thank you, students, for sharing your work with me and for your inspiration, vulnerability and courage. The need gotta be so deep! A special thank you to my friend and roomie Jenny Patton, a first-rate writer and a beloved kindred spirit. I treasure you.

Huge shout outs and hugs to my dear friend, the Drunken Master himself, Kiyoshi Nakazawa, for the beautiful image he gifted me for my book cover. He's on Etsy! Check him out! (www.luckynakazawa.com). Thank you to my friend Richard L. Reeder for sharing your Galapagos journal with me and for sharing your memories of our time there together, which meant so much to me as I was mourning the death of my father. Also thank you to my colleagues and friends at Pasadena City College, ULV, and to my SO CAL Poetry friends, all who have supported my writing and my voice: Don Campbell, Sherilyn Lee, Mike "the poet" Sonksen, Emily Fernandez, E. Kathy Kottaras, Akilah Brown, Gloria Horton, Cristina Salazar, Mikage Kuroki, Jane Hallinger, and the late Jane Dibbell - *we pray for peace, Jane*. A special thank you to my best friend, Terence Dobkins, whom I miss every day.

Gratitude to the following for monetary awards and fellowships for travel and time to write this book: University of La Verne; Pasadena City College; The Center for Contemporary Poetry & Poetics at Cal State LA, and especially Dr. Lauri Scheyer.

Special thanks to Miss Trudy and *The Porches Writing Retreat* for quiet time, rest, and inspiration as I revised these poems and wrote new ones.

Thanks to Jack Grapes and my Los Angeles Method
Writers— my friends . . . I had almost given up and you
made me stand up and, shaking, read it all out loud.

This book is dedicated to my grandmothers, Alice Rose Clement
Ogden and Irma Lee Cleavenger Wood, survivors, soothsayers,
strong-willed, tough warrior women. They both taught me
that a woman's voice matters, and so shout when you need to
shout and don't apologize for the sound you make. Let the earth
quake and the ground shake when you speak. Avid readers
and writers, they gave me their stories and gifts with urgency
and devotion and read my poems and stories with joy and
pride. I am blood of their blood. I am their granddaughter.

My parents loved me without limits: Marla Gregg, Ted Gregg,
Ronnie Ogden. This book is for you, too. Two people who have
parented me when I needed it - thank you for your love and for
the gift of your son in my life : Gene, Toni. For my girls Kayla and
Briana, and to my sister Nicole, who lived these poems with me.

Without my dear friend, teacher, and mentor Nancy Zafris,
this book wouldn't exist. There will never be enough
words to thank you for your mentoring, your friendship,
your belief in me and my writing, and your love.

Dear Mathew, I don't know if there's any way to measure
the fullness of my heart at your unwavering love.

To readers of poetry and also to the poets who never give up, to the
poets who can't stop, to the poets writing in closets and bleeding
all over their pages and standing up at open mics and reading out
loud, your voices and bodies shaking with fire, to you gathering in
circles to just say it, say it, keep going! Poetry is power, poetry is for
the people, poetry is life, poetry is love! To these readers and writers,
these brave revolutionaries, your names and your words are written
on my heart — my tribe, my family, for your friendship, for your
love, for your fight, for your poems, know that I keep you close here
in my heart and I whisper your words as prayer for a better world.

K.E. Ogden is a poet, essayist, book artist and educator. Kirsten grew up in Honolulu, Hawai'i and the SF Bay Area, and she spent almost every summer of her teen and twenty-something years in East Louisiana roaming the backroads with her grandmother. She loves writing on porches and still uses a typewriter for most things. A poet laureate of Gambier, Ohio, she teaches in Gambier each summer with the Kenyon Review Young Writer workshops and is one of the founding bloggers for *KRO: Kenyon Review Online*. A two-time judge for the Flannery O'Connor short fiction prize, Kirsten is also a former recipient of a Poetry Fellowship to Changsha, China from the CSULA Center for Contemporary Poetry & Poetics and a winner of the 2019 Academy of American Poets Henri Coulette Memorial Award for her poem "My Atoms Come from Those Stars." Her essays, poetry, and fiction have been published in *Brevity, KRO: Kenyon Review Online, Louisiana Literature, Streetlight Magazine, Windhover, andberbo* and elsewhere. Her digital quilt piece "My President: A Politics of Hope" was published at *UnstitchedStates.com* as part of a project curated by writer Gretchen Henderson. Kirsten is a certified Narrative Therapist and chairs the Creative Writing Committee at Pasadena City College. She believes that writing and poetry have the power to heal and to change the world. To learn more, visit her website at kirstenogden.com

www.ingramcontent.com/pod-product-compliance
Lightning Source LLC
Chambersburg PA
CBHW031818110426
42743CB00057B/986